The Church: Its Constitution And Government

Stuart Mitchell

THE CHURCH,

ITS CONSTITUTION AND GOVERNMENT.

Rev. STUART MITCHELL.

———————◆————————

PHILADELPHIA:
PRESBYTERIAN BOARD OF PUBLI.
NO. 821 CHESTNUT STREET.

PREFACE.

THIS little work makes no pretensions to origin-
ality. The author has simply tried to apprehend
the truth clearly, and tell it plainly. Those who
are familiar with the subject will perceive, perhaps
more clearly than himself, his obligations to others.
He does not affect to be indifferent in regard to the
questions at issue between different denominations,
and his preferences are plainly expressed in the
concluding chapters; but he has endeavoured to be
candid and charitable. And if it shall prove that
by any unjust, unfair, or erroneous statements he
has added in the least to those influences which
tend to sunder the professed followers of Christ, no
one will be more sorry for it than

THE AUTHOR

(3)

THE CHURCH,

ITS CONSTITUTION AND GOVERNMENT.

I.—THE CHURCH CHRIST'S BODY.

*Christ head over all for the church—Sense of
the word Church—The church one body—
Has a definite ideal plan and appropriate
life—Such is the Scriptural view—The ideal
church in process of erection—The unity of
the Spirit—The church not essentially a
visible organization—Evil of confounding the
true church with such an organization—A
practical question.*

THE Scriptures teach us that Christ is constituted Head over all things to the church, or
for the benefit of the church; and that the
church is his body, the fulness of him that
filleth all in all. Eph. i. 22, 23. This should

give us an exalted view of Christ and his church. He who a few hundred years ago walked sadly through the streets of Jerusalem, and sat weary by Jacob's well, and sweated blood in his agony, and staggered under the weight of his cross, and cried out in the hour of his trial, "My God, my God, why hast thou forsaken me?" administers the great scheme of divine government, which touches us at every point of our multiplex relations, and at every moment of our existence. It is administered by him for the same end that he had in view in suffering. As he loved his church and gave himself for it, as he purchased it with his own blood, so now he nourishes and defends it, and prepares it for its final presentation to himself as a bride adorned for her husband—a glorious church, without spot or wrinkle or any such thing. Eph. v. 25–27.

The welfare of the church being the great object for which the world is governed, we are concerned to know what the church is, so as to be able to determine our own relations to it; and this we propose to consider in the first place.   The word "church" in Scripture is evidently taken in various senses ; but the question we are now concerned with is, What is its meaning in the passages we have alluded to ?   It is not what is meant by *a* church, but what is meant by *the* church ?   What is that body of which Christ is the head ; which is his fulness or complement ; which he purchased with his own blood ; against which the gates of hell shall not prevail ?   Col. i. 18 ; Eph. i. 22, 23 ; Acts xx. 28 ; Matt. xvi. 18.   Is this body, which for convenience sake we shall call the true church, essentially an outward organization ?   Shall we say it is a visible body descended by succession from the Apostles, through whose offices alone grace can be obtained, and separation from which is inevitable ruin, whatever doctrines may be held and whatever virtues may be practised by those out of it ?   Shall we say it is nothing but the generalization by which we unite in one thought all the societies that assemble for Christian worship ?   We say neither of these. The true church, we say, is one body, but it is not essentially an outward organization. It is a real body, with a true bond of union, but the bond is an invisible one. It is not an outward and visible society, like the kingdom of Great Britain, yet it is not a mere generalization or form of thought.

That the true church is one body is expressed in Scripture frequently, as when the Apostle Paul says, "There is one body and one spirit, even as ye are called in one hope of your calling; one Lord, one faith, one baptism." Eph. iv. 4, 5. And in what is called the Apostles' Creed, the unity of the true church is expressed in saying, "I believe in the Holy Catholic church." It is not a number of holy churches, but one holy, catholic church.

In saying that the true church is one, we mean that it is one in all time. It is not one church before Christ and another church after Christ; but the martyr Stephen belonged to the same church as Moses; and we Christian Gentiles now belong to the same church as Abraham, inheriting the same promises of

divine favour. Acts vii. 38; Gal. iii. 29. It
is not one church on earth, and another in
heaven; not one church militant, and a
different church triumphant; but one church
in all time, past, present, and to come. The
true church is one in all lands. It is not the
English church, the Dutch church, the Scotch
church, or the American church, but the
church of Christ. It is not the Romish, the
Episcopal, the Lutheran, or the Reformed
church; it is not any of the various denominations of Independents or Baptists or Meth-
odists or Quakers; it is not the sum total of
these; but it is one body.

When the true church is described as one
body, we allude to the fact that a body has a
definite form and size, and is actuated throughout by one spirit or life. The church in the
view of the divine mind is a complete body,
not an accidental collection of saved souls,
but a perfectly definite though immensely vast
number of individuals arranged in their re-
spective positions. To us, whose existence is
passed in time, the church is not complete.

The Lord is daily adding some living stones to the growing edifice. With us it is a matter of uncertainty who shall form this living temple, or how many, except as we make certain of our own place in the building. But with God there is no such uncertainty. The completed church stands before his view as if it were already finished, every stone in its place polished and fitted. Every member of this church is already saved, or certainly will be. The faultless bride shall lack no perfection of excellence or beauty in the day of her presentation to her Lord.

That this view of the church is presented in Scripture, will be granted by every candid and attentive reader of holy writ. It will be remembered that the word church is also used in other senses, but we speak of that church which has the assurance of salvation, and for whose benefit Christ is governing the world. The Scriptures frequently speak of this church as Christ's body. Paul says, " So we being many are one body in Christ, and every one members one of another." " For as the body is one and hath many members, and all the members of that one body being many are one body, so also is Christ." "Now ye are the body of Christ and members in particular." He tells us that the teachers of the church are given for the edifying of the body of Christ, and speaks of our growing up into him in all things, which is the head, even Christ; " From whom the whole body fitly joined together and compacted by that which every joint supplieth, according to the effectual working in the measure of every part, maketh increase of the body to the edifying of itself in love." Rom. xii. 5 ; 1 Cor. xii. 12, 27 ; Eph. iv. 16.

He describes Christ as the head of the body, the church ; speaks of enduring afflictions for Christ's body's sake, which is the church ; and calls Christ's body " the fulness" or complement, signifying that Christ and his church constitute a glorious whole, requiring both parts for its completion. Col. i. 18, 24. Eph. i. 23. Peter speaks of living stones that are built up a spiritual house. 1 Pet. ii. 5. It

is not an unarranged heap, but an edifice, built
according to a plan, in which every stone is
thought of and provided for while yet in the
quarry.

The apostles regarded this edifice as not
yet finished. Paul saw it growing as each believer was called out of the darkness and sin-
fulness of his natural estate, and took the
place assigned him in the plan. To the
Ephesians he says, "Ye are built upon the
foundation of the apostles and prophets, Jesus
Christ himself being the chief corner-stone;
in whom all the building fitly framed together
groweth unto an holy temple in the Lord : in
whom ye also are builded together for an habita-
tion of God through the Spirit. Eph. ii. 20–22.
Christ also spoke of his church as not yet
complete, thus implying an ideal plan to which
it is to be conformed when it arrives at completion. He represented it as a flock that had
been given him, whose members, however,
were yet straying, and were hereafter to be
gathered : "Other sheep I have which 'are
not of this fold, them also I must bring."

He spoke of the certainty of their being gathered and safely kept. To the Jews he said, " But ye believe not, because ye are not of my sheep, as I said unto you. My sheep hear my voice, and I know them, and they follow me; and I give unto them eternal life, and they shall never perish, neither shall any pluck them out of my hand." Though as yet out of his fold, and not gathered to him, he calls them his sheep, because his Father had given them to him. He says, " My Father which gave them me is greater than all, and none is able to pluck them out of my Father's hand." John. x. 16, 26, 27, 28, 29. To assure the Jews that although they had seen him and believed not, he should nevertheless have disciples, he said, " All that the Father giveth me shall come to me, and him that cometh to me, I will in no wise cast out." He further declares it is his Father's will that of all which he has given him he should lose nothing, but should raise it up at the last day. At the last supper, he prayed not only for his actual followers, but also for others yet to

2

believe : " Neither pray I for these alone, but
for them also that shall believe on me through
their word." He prays for them also as those
who had been given him : " Father, I will that
they also whom thou hast given me be with
me where I am." John vi. 37, 39 ; xvii. 20,
24. The Captain of our salvation, looking
down through the ages that were to intervene
before his second coming, saw the whole
process by which his army should be enlisted
and organized, and fitted to follow him in his
last glorious triumph over the powers of darkness. This he regarded as the recompense
of his toil ; even as Isaiah had prophesied,
" He shall see of the travail of his soul and
shall be satisfied ;" " He shall see his seed."
Is. liii. 10, 11. He spoke of this as the
design of his exaltation : " Father, the hour is
come ; glorify thy Son that thy Son also may
glorify thee, as thou hast given him power
over all flesh, that he should give eternal life
to as many as thou hast given him." John
xvii. 1, 2. This passage of his prayer may
be compared with Paul's saying that God gave

him to be head over all things to the church.
Being head over all things to or for the church,
is having power over all flesh to give eternal
life to as many as are given him. The scriptural idea of the true church in its complete-
ness, is the whole body of those who are given
to Christ by the Father ; to whom the Son in
due time gives eternal life ; whom none can
pluck out of the good Shepherd's hand ; and
of whom he has engaged to lose none, but to
raise it up at the last day.

But as this church is not yet completed, and
will not be until the end of the world, the
actually existing true church is but part of it,
and must be defined within a narrower limit.
The complete idea is not fully actualized.
The building is still in process of erection ; it
is, so to speak, under contract. So far as it
is already erected, it consists of those who,
having been given by the Father to the Son,
have been actually united to him by the Holy
Spirit. In this church every member is regenerated by the Holy Ghost, and thus all
are constituted one body by partaking of one

spirit. " By one spirit we are all baptized
into one body." " There is one body and one
spirit, even as ye are called in one hope of
your calling." 1 Cor. xii. 13; Eph. iv. 4. The
true church is one in all ages, because the
Holy Spirit which dwells in every member as
the cause of union, is the same in every age.
It is the same body in all lands, for the same
Spirit works in the hearts of believers in every
clime.   National, sectional, or denominational
prejudices in imperfect believers may hinder
the manifestations of this unity, and yet the
church is one.   Neither time nor distance can
break the circuit of sympathy.   The true
believer in America feels that he belongs to
the same body as the persecuted Christian of
India or Madagascar, however separated by
circumstantial differences.   This unity of the
Spirit, as the Apostle Paul calls it, is the true
unity of the church; and that church which
possesses this unity, that body which in the
creed is called " the Holy Catholic church, the
communion of saints," that church alone is the

true church, the body of Christ, for whose welfare the world is governed.

It has been said above, that this church does not consist of any outward organization, or of any number of them. Without under-valuing the outward organization which bears the name of church, let us distinguish between it and that true church which it represents. The latter is a company whose members are known only to God. For this reason it is often called the *invisible* church. Not that its members are invisible, for they are visible men and women and children; not that it does not show itself by its works, for it is a city set on a hill that cannot be hid; but that it is united not by a visible organization, but by an in-visible bond, the operation of the Holy Spirit. "The Holy Catholic church" is not, as Romanists would make it, the company of professing Christians, pious or not pious, living under a certain form of church govern-ment, but "the communion of saints." When any would claim that their organization is the church, the body of Christ, we rebut the claim,

2*

not by asserting that our organization is the
body of Christ, but by asserting that the
church to which the promises belong, in which
every member is safe, and out of which there
is no salvation, is independent of all external
organization.   When ritualists argue that in
Scripture the church is spoken of and addressed
as a visible society of professing Christians,
that the Jewish church was a visible organization, and to it were given promises and
covenants, and that the Christian church is
divinely provided with laws and offices and
terms of admission ; we answer, that when the
church is addressed as a visible society, or a
visible society addressed as the church, it is
on the same principle that professed Christians
are addressed as believers.   A man who pro-
fesses to be a Christian may be regarded and
treated as such, without our asserting or en-
dorsing the truth of his profession ; and in
like manner a body of men that profess
Christianity may be regarded and treated as
a part of the body of Christ.   The ancient
Jewish church was called Israel, and addressed

as the people of God, because they so professed to be; but Paul says "they are not all Israel which are of Israel, and he is not a Jew which is one outwardly." Rom. ix. 6; ii. 28. The visible church, it is true, has an organization with laws and offices according to divine appointment; and the visible Hebrew church had these with covenants and promises addressed to it. But if giving laws and offices to a church, or addressing covenants and promises to it, constituted it the body of Christ, then the body of Christ may apostatize, for the Hebrew organization rejected the Messiah and persecuted his disciples. Our government gives a certain privilege of preemption in buying land, to actual settlers. It directs the mode in which the claim of preemption shall be made, and appoints officers to enrol the claimants. If now in giving certain advice or directions to these claimants, it should address them indiscriminately, according to their profession, as actual settlers, it would not follow that the privilege of preemption belonged to all who were enrolled, and simply because they were enrolled. There might be many claimants who could not prove that they were actual settlers according to the requirements of the law; on the other hand, supposing our government were administered with something less of human imperfection, it might secure the privilege to many actual settlers who had been unable to make the pre-emption claim in the manner directed; and these cases would be discriminated when the time came for examining the proof, though no such discrimination would be made or needed in giving the advice. So the visible church, as it represents the church, is addressed as the church; yet it consists of the tares and the wheat, and the wheat alone has the promise of being gathered into the garner.

In fact, none of the organizations that claim to be *the* church, answers to the scriptural description of the body of Christ. All the members of Christ's body are truly pious believers, but the largest charity cannot admit this of any of these organizations. Those that make the largest claims show most clearly that the claims are unfounded. This, indeed, is the tendency of confounding the visible church with the body of Christ. If the visible organization is the true church, then, as Christ's body is holy, all the members of the society are such, and all out of it are not. As Christ saves all his members and none other, all the members of this society must be saved, and all others lost. As Christ has promised his Spirit to guide his church into the knowledge of the truth, this society is infallibly right as to the doctrines necessary to salvation. Whatever, therefore, secures admission and continuance in the society must be the cardinal virtues and duties. The main thing is to get into the organization and keep in it. The power of the keys becomes not merely a power to declare the terms on which God will remit sin, but the power to admit to heaven or cast into hell, according as those who hold it may receive or reject the applicant for church membership. As the outward organization can take cognizance only of the outward conduct, the most important duties must be the outward observances enjoined by the church; and the weightier matters of the law, judgment, mercy, and faith, become of less importance. Regeneration becomes baptism; penitence, penance; and faith, submission to ecclesiastical superiors.

These, and such as these, are the logical consequences of regarding any visible organization as *the* church, the body of Christ. However modestly the claims of any particular organization to be so regarded may be put forth at first; however plausible the plan may seem which proposes to unite the many sects of professors into one communion, which shall be *the* church; however charitable it may seem to receive into this church people of all shades of belief and all kinds of practice, it is well to beware; for underneath this lie the seeds of that monstrous corruption and that tremendous spiritual tyranny, which have distinguished the church of Rome.

Such is the tendency of human nature, that, with all the teaching of Scripture, men can hardly be kept from supposing that if they

are only members of a visible church organization, they are safe, and that if zealous
for its spread and growth, they are pious.
There is the same tendency outside of the
visible church as in it. Unconverted persons,
when invited to enter Christ's church, answer
by objections against the organizations that
represent it, or against professors of religion
who misrepresent it. It is highly desirable,
therefore, to see clearly that the true church
is not an outward organization, but the communion of saints, whose unity is the unity of
the Spirit. A clear apprehension of this
point clears the way of much sophistry concerning the church.

Above all, it is desirable to belong to the
true church, and it is well to inquire how we
stand related to it. Do I belong to that body
of which Christ is the head? Am I on Christ's
side, and he on mine, in the great contest
against evil? Or am I against Christ, taking
part with those powers that he is to conquer
and punish?

II.—THE VISIBLE CHURCH.

The word Church also applied in Scripture to a visible organization—Ecclesia and Synagogue—The Christian church adopts the name Ecclesia—Its title to the name—The visible church is properly the representative of the true church—The true church must make itself visible—This is the natural effect of the Christian disposition—It is necessary to the work of the church—The visible church is established by God—Covenant with Abraham—The visible church under Moses—In Christ's day—Recognized and modified by Christ and his Apostles.

WHILE the word "Church" in some passages of Scripture means the communion of saints, the company of those who have been given to Christ by the Father, in other passages it signifies the visible organization of professed believers in Christ. The word Church in our version of the New Testament is the translation of the Greek word *Ecclesia.* This word was familiar to the Jews as denoting the pro-

fessed people of God in their organized
capacity. It was used in their Greek version
of the Old Testament to signify the congregation of the Lord. In Heb. ii. 12, we have the
words of David in the 22nd Psalm quoted
thus, "I will declare thy name unto my
brethren; in the midst of *the church* will I
sing praise unto thee." Luke, in giving the
words of Stephen concerning Moses, says,
"This is he that was in *the church*, in the
wilderness with the angel that spake to him
in the Mount Sinai." Acts vii. 38. The word
being thus familiar to the Jews, when Christ
said in reference to dealing with an offender,
"If he neglect to hear thee, tell it to the
church," Matt. xviii. 17, they readily understood him to refer to what is called in our
English version of the Old Testament, "the
congregation of the Lord"—the professed
people of God in their organized capacity.

At this time, however, another word was in
common use to designate the existing religious
organization. The Jews being widely scattered
through the Roman Empire, and accustomed ·

3

to meet on Sabbath days for worship, needed
and had an organization independent of the
civil government under which they lived.
Their assemblies were called by the Greek
name Synagogues, *i. e.* congregations. The
name Synagogue was also given to the place
of assembling, and to the organization that
met there. Each synagogue had a number of
Elders to administer its affairs, one of whom
was called the Chief of the Synagogue, and
also a minister or servant, corresponding
nearly to our sexton. These synagogues were
found in all the considerable cities of the
Roman Empire. There are mentioned in
Scripture the synagogues of Damascus, to
whom Saul took letters from the High Priest
at Jerusalem. Acts ix. 2. In Jerusalem we
read of the synagogue of the Libertines, and
Cyrenians, and Alexandrians, and of the
people of Cilicia and proconsular Asia. Acts
vi. 9. The Rabbins say that Jerusalem con-
tained 460. The word Synagogue had thus
come into common use to denote the existing
religious organization of the Jews.

When the Jews had rejected the Messiah, a name was needed for the Christian organization, to characterize it and to distinguish it from that of the unbelieving Jews. The word Ecclesia (church) was the one they had been used to apply to the ancient people of God, and it had been used also by our Saviour in reference to his kingdom; " Upon this rock I will build my church." Matt. xvi. 18. What more natural than that the Christians should apply it to their society! They thus expressed the fact that their body was not essentially a new one, but the old church of God which Moses led in the wilderness and David sang praises in ; while at the same time it was distinguished from the Synagogue, which had rejected the Messiah. The body thus designated is assumed throughout the New Testament to be the successor of the Old Testament church.

We have here a scriptural example of a transfer of the title and prerogatives of the visible church from one organization to another. Whence did the society formed by Christ and

his Apostles obtain a right to the name church?
How did it appear that it was the true successor
of the "church that was in the wilderness?"
It could only be because it now represented
the true church, the body of Christ; while the
Jewish organization did not. It was not
because it had the succession of an outward
organization, for those who rejected the Messiah
and gave him to be crucified—"the Elders of
the people," who with the Scribes and Priests
took counsel against Jesus to put him to death
—these had the regular succession. When
Paul on his missionary journey established a
church and ordained elders in every city, since
the synagogue would not always, and perhaps
not often, as a body receive Jesus as the
Messiah, a new organization was needed, and
was made—a society of the professed people
of God living under the government of Elders.
In such cases the new organization was a
schism from the old; and of the two bodies,
alike in organization, the older one had the
regular succession, yet the younger one claimed
and kept the title of Ecclesia, church.

As has been indicated, this can be explained
only upon the principle that the visible church
is the *representative* of the true church, the
body of Christ; and therefore a society is
properly called the visible church which well
and truly represents the company of God's
chosen. The Jewish organization in the time
of the Apostles, though it had a proper form
of government, and ordinances of divine worship, divinely given, and a regular succession
from the body that had been recognized by
God in various ways as the visible church, was
nevertheless no longer entitled to the name,
because it did not truly represent the invisible
church, the communion of saints. So any
society now calling itself a church is entitled
to the name just so far as it represents the
true church, the body of Christ. If it could
be made to appear that there is now a society
in the world descended by regular succession
from the Apostles, it would not only not make
it the true church, in which alone is salvation,
but it would not even entitle it to the name
of *a* church, except so far as it could be shown

3 *

to be a true representative of Christ's body. As a professing Christian may be a real Christian or may not, and is entitled to the name of Christian just so far and so long as he appears to be a Christian; so a company of professed Christians, organized for church purposes, is entitled to the name of a visible church just so far as they appear to be visible Christians, of which appearance we are to judge with all charity.

We have thus far taken for granted that there ought to be a visible church, that is, an external organization of professing Christians representative of the true or invisible church; and we have done so in accordance with Scripture.

From the nature of the case the true church of Christ must show itself. Its members are visible men and women, who have experienced an influence of the Holy Ghost that has visible results; and whatever they are, they must be seen and known as such. If there be any principle in the heart, it must come out in the life. "I believed, therefore have I spoken,"

said the Psalmist; "we also believe and therefore speak," says Paul, 2 Cor. iv. 13. He
that believes must speak by word or action.
Christ's followers are required to show themselves. He says that his disciples "are the
light of the world." As a city that is set on a
hill cannot be hid, or as a light set in a
candlestick gives light to all in the house, so
his disciples are not to hide their light under
a bushel, but to let it shine before men, that
they may see and glorify their Father which is
in heaven. The Apostle Peter says that
Christians "are called out of darkness into
marvellous light, that they may show forth the
praises of him that has called them." Matt. v.
13–16; 1 Pet. ii. 9. All this must make the
church visible.

As Christians have views of the way of
salvation different from the rest of the world,
different principles of action, different ends to
gain; as they find that the world generally
does not respect what they regard most, and
finds pleasure in occupations distasteful to
them, they must unavoidably separate from

it. According to our Saviour's prediction, the world hates them as it hated him. John xv. 18, 19. If it does not hate their persons, as men and women, it hates their attachment to Christ and their dislike of its sinful pursuits. Even though Christians seek no separation from the world, the world will soon separate from them if they are consistent, as Christ told his disciples, "Blessed are ye when men shall hate you, and when they shall separate you from their company. . . . . for the Son of man's sake." Luke vi. 22. Furthermore, as Christians find they have something in common with each other, the same sense of sin, the same dependence on Christ, and the same wish to obey his commands, they will spontaneously come together and make themselves known to each other. In a state of society where the gospel has brought all to some extent under its influence, these results will not be as plainly seen as in infidel and pagan communities, where the line between believers and unbelievers is more definitely marked; but the natural effect of Christianity, never-

theless, is to form the followers of Christ into
a separate society for purposes in which the
world feels little or no interest, or to which
it is avowedly hostile.

This is not only the natural effect of the
Christian disposition when fairly developed,
but it is necessary to the successful execution
of the work that is committed to the followers
of Christ.   They are entrusted with the work
of helping each other's faith, maintaining the
knowledge and remembrance of Christ in the
world, and preaching his gospel to every
creature. 1 Thess. v. 11, 14; 1 Cor. xi. 24,
25; Mark xvi. 15.   This cannot be done
efficiently without organization.   If there were
no visible church, there would be none set
apart to watch for souls, none ordained to
preach the gospel, no remembering Christ in
the sacraments.   As in every department of
active life—in politics, in science, and in art—
association and organization are found necessary to increase the interest and zeal of individuals in particular causes, and to give it
suitable direction; so religious association and

organization are the means of enlivening zeal
for the glory of God and also of assisting individuals to overcome temptation and to re-
cover themselves out of the snare of the
Devil.

It is equally necessary for preaching the
gospel to the heathen. Every Christian, and
indeed every soul that hears the gospel, is
under obligation to take part in preaching it
to the whole world. The commission left by
Christ is binding upon all, and his true followers must acknowledge the obligation. But
since it is a physical impossibility for all to
go to the heathen, the self-denial of this work
can be assumed by all only by sending their
representatives; and this can be done only by
organization. There must be some mode of
choosing the representatives, and of examining
those that offer themselves, else Christians
might be sending men to preach against Christ;
and there must also be some means of secur-
ing a support for the missionary while he is
labouring in the gospel, all which implies organization. In saying that organization is

necessary, God's ability to dispense with it if he sees fit, is of course not denied; but it is meant that he has seen fit to make it, in all ordinary cases, necessary to success in this work that his professed people should organize.

Besides that an external organization is the natural effect of Christian faith and is made necessary in the Divine Providence to accomplish the work of gathering in the church and preparing it for glory, it is to be added that God has himself established the visible church. He has done so, not only by making it the duty of his people to confess Christ before the world, which must of itself lead to separation from the world and association with each other, but also by still more direct means. The true church has existed wherever believers did from the days of Adam and Eve, and it had visibility—signs to distinguish it from the rest of the world. The conduct of Abel and Enoch was a witness for their faith, and their sacrifices were a divinely appointed ordinance of worship. But God gave the church a more

complete visible organization in the family of
Abraham. He gave Abraham an outward
sign by which the members of the visible organization should be distinguished from the
rest of the world, as professedly in covenant
with him. The better to secure the perpetuity
of the church, the same covenant stood ever
in force with the same seal, and the genera-
tions were born and brought up under it,
Abraham agreeing not only for himself but
also for his seed that the Lord should be their
God and that they should be his people. Gen.
vii. 7–14. This was the visible church. It
was not the body of Christ, for its members
do not appear to have been all pious believers ;
but it was its divinely ordained and only representative on earth.

As God had given one outward sign to
Abraham to distinguish the members of the
church from the rest of the world, and to
signify that they had professedly entered into
covenant with him, so he gave another to
Moses, which, unlike circumcision, was to be
repeated every year. Ex. xii ; Deut. xvi. 1–8.

Whoever ate the passover thereby signified his adherence to the true religion. No stranger might eat of it who did not first profess his faith in the God of Israel by being circumcised. Whoever wished to express his disbelief in Jehovah, or his attachment to the worship of any other God, need only neglect the Passover, and he would thereby signify his breaking the covenant of the fathers and his separation from the church. The law said, "But the man that is clean and is not in a journey and forbeareth to keep the passover, even the same soul shall be cut off from among his people ;" and again, " Whosoever eateth that which is leavened, even that soul shall be cut off from the congregation of Israel, whether he be a stranger or born in the land." Num. ix. 13; Ex. xii. 19. Here then was an outward organization with outward signs of membership, by which the people professed their faith in the true God and obedience to him; and this outward organization with its signs was established by God himself. He further gave it ordinances of divine worship, a

4

sanctuary, sacred times, and a consecrated priesthood. When it became corrupt and disobedient, he sent prophets to rebuke it, and raised up pious kings to reform it. He gave it into captivity for its sin, and brought it back again according to his promise, dealing with it all the time as an organization of professed believers, the representative, though often very imperfect, of the spiritual Israel. If any should refuse to call this a church because it was connected with the state and embraced the whole nation under its government, they should also deny the existence of a church in most of the Protestant states of Europe. The Scriptures however call it the church. Acts vii. 38 ; Heb. ii. 12.

This visible organization was existing when Christ came. Hitherto as the church had been mainly confined to one nation, the visible church and the nation had lived under the same government. Hereafter the church was to go into all nations and work its way in spite of the opposition of heathen powers ; and so, providence had been preparing the way

for a separation of church and state. When
Christ came, whose kingdom, though in the
line of David, was not to be a kingdom of this
world, the separation was already partly ac-
complished. In Judea the supreme civil power
had passed into the hands of the heathen,
while the ecclesiastical power remained with the
Jewish synagogue; and throughout the Roman
empire the Jews, though destitute of civil
power, carried with them their religious organization. This was christianized where the
majority of the synagogue would receive Jesus
as the Christ; and where they would not, it
served as a model for a new organization.
This may explain why more was not said in
Scripture about the details of church organization and government; the early converts
had been familiarized with these details in the
synagogue.

Christ and his apostles, however, did not
leave the existence of the visible church to
depend on the spontaneous feeling of the converts, nor to be secured by the necessities of
their work, nor even by their Jewish habits.

Christ recognized the visible church. He gave it baptism and the Lord's supper (in place of circumcision and the passover) as the outward signs by which his followers should profess their connection with him and with each other, as separate from the world. He also gave directions for dealing with offenders. Matt. xxviii. 19; Luke xxii. 19; Matt. xviii. 15–17. The apostles when they gathered converts organized them. They told the people to choose the officers, and then ordained them by the laying on of hands. They ordained Elders in every city, and provided for the future by giving directions as to the qualifications of the church officers. They commanded the people not to neglect the assembling of themselves together; and they taught them in reference to conducting public worship, supporting their religious teachers, and assisting their brethren in want. We have apostolic directions also as to the exclusion of immoral members, and their reception upon repentance. Acts xiv. 23; Tit. i. 5; 1 Tim. iii; Titus i. 5–9; Heb. x. 25; 1 Cor.

ix. 11–14 ; 2 Cor. viii ; 1 Cor. v. 11 ; 2 Thess.
iii. 6, 14, 15 ; 2 Cor. ii. 7.

In all this they were establishing a visible
church. Baptism and the Lord's supper could
not designate the members of the true church,
the body of Christ, but only the members of
that society which is its outward representative. The Elders or Bishops had under their
care all who voluntarily placed themselves
under it, though of these there were doubtless
many that were not true believers. That
some such did belong to these apostolic
churches is as plain as that some such belonged to the church that was with Moses in
the wilderness. The apostle John speaks
of some that " went out from us, but they were
not of us ;" and, according to Paul, there
were even teachers who preached another
gospel, and whom he wished out of the church ;
" I would they were even cut off which trouble
you." 1 John ii. 19 ; Gal. v. 12. Yet as these
societies were representative of the true church
they received its name ; and Paul addresses
his letters to the " churches of Galatia," and

4 *

to the "church of God which is at Corinth," even when pointing out faults inconsistent with Christian character. It is the expressed will of God, therefore, as well as the dictate of Christian prudence and the result of Christian feeling, that there should be a visible church to represent on earth the true flock of Christ.

III.—THE DUTY OF UNITING WITH THE VISIBLE CHURCH.

A duty of all to whom the gospel comes—Most plainly the duty of Christians—No exceptions—Evils of neglecting this duty—Sense of unworthiness no disqualification for membership—Objections from the imperfection of the visible church—Objection from the number of sects.

FROM what has been said it follows that it is the duty of all to whom the gospel comes, not only to receive Christ as their Saviour with faith and penitence, but also to join the visible church and promote its purity and prosperity to the best of their ability. We cannot indeed expect that those who refuse the first duty of receiving Christ, will discharge the next duty of confessing, following and serving him in his visible church; nor do we wish that those who refuse to enter the true church of Christ by faith, should enter the visible church by profession. But we wish to remind all, the ungodly as well as the pious, of their double obligation.

Those especially who wish to obey and serve Christ, should remember that it is their duty to belong to the visible church. For if it be not the duty of every follower of Christ, then it cannot be shown to be the duty of any; for Christ makes no distinction among his followers in this respect. If you may be excused from joining it, then all others may. If it is not your duty, then it is the duty of no one, and then the visible church is destroyed. Then there will be no ministry, no sacraments, no watch and care of souls, no missions. Christ's disciples, instead of obeying his command to let their light shine, will hide it under a bushel; instead of receiving

gratefully his gift of pastors and teachers for
the edifying of the body of Christ, they will
allow the whole system of instruction to cease;
instead of obeying them that have the rule
over them and watch for their souls, they will
have no Christian rulers at all, nor any to
watch for their souls; instead of obeying his
charge to preach the gospel to every creature,
they will not even secure its preaching to
their neighbours. This total overthrow of
the divinely appointed arrangements for the
edification of the body of Christ, is the legitimate result of denying that it is the duty of
every follower of his to join the visible organization of his people. It is true that the
withdrawing or witholding of one Christian
will not destroy it, yet this is not because it is
not the tendency of the action. It may not
be in our power to do a great deal either for
the church or against it; but we are as fully
responsible for what we can do and for the
tendency of our course, as if we were able to
decide its whole destiny by our single act.

It is not uncommon for persons to think

that some peculiarity in their circumstances makes their case an exception. But Christ took into view as strong a case as persecution for his sake, and even opposition from near friends—a man's foes those of his own household—and yet he made no exception when he said, " But whosoever shall deny me before men, him will I also deny before my Father which is in heaven." In fact, he added, " He that taketh not his cross and followeth after me, is not worthy of me." Matt. x. 28-89. When the early Christians, exposed on every hand to odium and even persecution, neglected the assembling of themselves together, they were admonished against such neglect by apostolic authority. And there is much reason to fear that those Christians who withhold themselves from the church, and are indifferent to its welfare (if such Christians there be), while they hinder the cause of Christ, will also suffer great loss themselves, and may be creating a need for severe chastisement to bring them into the way of duty.

. The Christian who does not separate himself from the world by uniting with the visible church, cannot but suffer loss. He deprives himself of the blessing that God is wont to bestow upon those who in faith seal their covenant with him in the solemn sacraments of his church. He continues to stand in slippery places, where he must resist the full power of Satan and the world to drag him down, while he makes no use of the guards and helps that God has ordained for his people by means of their communion and fellowship. He is in an enemy's country, but instead of connecting himself with the army he straggles alone as if among friends, inviting the enemy to cut him off, and tempting God to leave him to his fate. He keeps a door of retreat from God's service always open, inviting him to give up the struggle, when he ought to silence temptation by cutting off all possibility of retreat. Living thus, he cannot have full confidence in claiming the promises. He cannot say as David said, " I have not refrained my lips, O Lord, thou knowest. I have not hid thy righteousness within my heart; I have declared

thy faithfulness and thy salvation. I have
not concealed thy loving-kindness and thy
truth from the great congregation;" and
therefore he cannot say with David's confidence, " Withhold not thou thy tender mercies
from me, O Lord; let thy loving-kindness and
thy truth continually preserve me." Ps. xl.
9–11. The whole tendency of his course is
to bring on lukewarmness, indifference, and
backsliding. One most valuable means of
grace is labouring for Christ's cause; but he
cuts himself off in great measure from the
opportunity to do this, if he remains separate
from any visible organization of Christians,
when he might unite with one.

As such a Christian does not take an open
and decided stand for Christ and his church,
he may thus become a great stumbling block,
hindering the conversion of others. Christians
are discouraged for want of his help, and the
ungodly are encouraged by his seeming to
countenance their rejection of Christ and his
claims. The good that he may do to the
bodies of men cannot balance the failure to do

good to their souls. Even in his own family
his desire for the piety and salvation of his
children is counteracted, and his efforts neu-
tralized by his position. If he hides his religion from the world and the church, he
cannot well profess it in the bosom of his
family. When he would speak with his family
about their souls or pray with them, his mouth
is stopped by the thought of his own real or
seeming inconsistency, and his desire to discharge the duty dies for want of exercise.
What wonder if his children, growing up
without any recognition of their peculiar relation to God as the offspring of his people,
should take no interest in the church and be
disinclined to its services !

It may be objected by one who looks to
Christ for salvation, and wishes to honour him,
" I am not worthy to join the visible church.
I fear I should bring discredit upon it." We
answer, Any one is worthy to join the visible
church, who, feeling himself a guilty and helpless sinner, and looking to Christ alone for
salvation, takes him for Teacher, Ruler, and

Mediator. The visible church is a company professing themselves to be lost sinners by nature, and so unworthy that they can only hope for salvation through the merits of Christ. The visible church is intended as a help to the weak disciple. God has graciously established it for the benefit of those who feel their need of help to live a Christian life. Of this we may be sure that Christ is not so much dishonoured by the failings of those who feel their weakness, and are ready to repent of their faults, and to confess their need of Christ's merits to atone for them, as he is by the unbelief of those who looking only or chiefly to their own strength, decline obedience to his commands in dependence on his strength. But the main consideration is that we have no discretion in the matter. Christ knows better than we do what is best for his cause. Our duty is to take our place in the rank of his followers, trusting to him for courage and strength and victory in the day of battle.

Sometimes an objection is drawn from the imperfection of the church. The excuse is

5

not so much "I am not worthy to join the church," as "the church is not worthy to have me join it." Excluding cases where the visible church may be peculiarly corrupt, we may suppose that the objection ordinarily proceeds either from a want of proper humility and self-knowledge, or from a mistaken view of the visible church. It may be that the objector does not feel himself a poor sinner who needs all the help God's ordinances afford to keep him in the path of duty. The purest church on earth is a company of very weak and unworthy sinners; and if he does not regard himself as such, the church is no place for him. He is too good for it, even as he is too good to be saved by Christ; for "they that be whole need not a physician, but they that are sick." Or he may have fallen into the error of supposing that the visible church must be made to coincide exactly with the invisible, and that every one must be cast out who does not show plainly that he is beyond doubt a true Christian. Besides that true Christians are sinners, and are no more to be

kept out of the church for every failing than
scholars are to be kept out of school for their
ignorance, it is to be remembered that Christ
does not allow us to purge the visible church
of all who do not fully satisfy us that they
are true Christians. As we cannot discern
the hearts of men, we are not to try rooting
out the tares lest we root out the wheat with
them.

If any Christian is disposed to excuse himself by this plea for neglecting the visible
church, let him remember that Christ divides
men into two parties, them that are for him
and them that are against him, the church and
the world. Matt. xii. 30; Mark ix. 40. The
former is represented by the visible church;
and the man stands outwardly on the world's
side, whatever he may be in heart, who does
not stand with the church. If the church is
not good enough for him, is the world any
better? If the visible church does not well
enough represent the cause of Christ, does the
visible world represent it at all? The truth
is that, while he does not allow Christ's visible

kingdom to claim him as one of its members, he does not prevent Satan's visible kingdom from strengthening itself in opposition to God by his example.

The number of sects is sometimes objected, but to a true Christian this certainly leaves so much the less reason for staying out of the church. If all the army wore one uniform, fought with one weapon only, spoke the same dialect precisely, the recruit might find some unpleasant feature to hinder his enlisting. But when it is divided into companies, each differently armed and equipped, so that not only his conscience but even his tastes and prejudices may be suited, he must be sadly disinclined to the service if he cannot find a place somewhere.

We repeat then, that as there is on earth a visible church, representative of the true church, the body of Christ; and as such a church is not only demanded by true Christian feeling, and requisite to the completion of the work of redemption, but has also been established by divine authority, it is the immediate duty

Of every one who looks to Christ for salvation, to join it, and strive not only to reap the benefits it affords, but also to promote its prosperity by his prayers and efforts.

IV.—THE CHARACTERISTICS OF THE VISIBLE CHURCH.

The faith of the true church is to be represented in the visible church—The obedience of the true church is to be represented—Discipline not intended to make the visible church identical with the true—Outward conduct the object of discipline—Visible church to be separate from the world—The unity of the true church is to be represented in the visible church—Limitation of the principle—Uniformity not unity—The sin of schism—Visible church not to be needlessly divided—Union gives efficiency—It is scriptural.

As the visible church is representative of the invisible, it should represent faithfully its prominent characteristics.   These are faith in Christ, obedience to Christ, and the unity of believers.

5 *

Faith in Christ is the main characteristic of
the true church. It is the foundation of
obedience to Christ and the bond of union
among Christians. No one becomes a true
Christian save as he believes Christ to be
what he claims to be. The Christian believes
all Christ's words, accepting him as his
Prophet as well as his Priest and King. It is
by his faith above all that he is distinguished
from other men. To the unbelieving Jews
Christ said, "My sheep hear my voice."
"Ye believe not, because ye are not of my
sheep." John x. 26, 27.

The first requisite in the visible church, then,
in order to represent the true church, is a
true creed, pure doctrine, faithful and correct
teaching. The world, as is natural, seeks to
depreciate and ridicule attention to matters
of belief, and some Christians are weak enough
to be misled by the device. But the history
of the church in all ages confirms the deduc-
tion from the nature of the church itself, that
a true creed is the bulwark of the visible
church, as a living faith is the very breath of

the church invisible.   The very efforts of the
world to depreciate and ridicule doctrine as
unimportant, show their instinctive sense of its
importance to the safety and progress of true
religion.

By the creed we mean the belief of the
church duly recognized and taught.   A visible
church may have a true creed in its books,
and yet be far from representing well the
faith of the true church, because its members
may assent to the creed in words without
heartily believing it.   It of course does not
follow that a society with a false creed can
properly represent the true church.   There
may indeed be a great difference in the pre-
cision and fulness of the creeds of different
bodies, all of which may be considered representative of the true church.   In proportion
to the intelligence and unity of a body the
statement of what it believes may be made
more full and precise.   But all must agree
that the profession of belief by which the
visible church is united should be a profession
of the belief of revealed truth.   As disbelief

of revealed truth excludes from salvation, so
a profession of disbelief should exclude from
the visible church. Says the Apostle John,
"If any come unto you and bring not this
doctrine, receive him not into your house,
neither bid him God speed." 2 John 10.

Another characteristic of the true church
is *obedience to Christ*. Says Christ, "My
sheep hear my voice, and I know them, and
they follow me." "If a man love me he will
keep my words." The Apostle Paul says,
"The church is subject unto Christ." John x.
27; John xiv. 21, 23; Eph. v. 24. Obedience, therefore, should characterize the visible
church. It should maintain the preaching of
the gospel and seek to preach it to every
creature, for so Christ has commanded. It
should maintain the administration of the
sacraments according to his directions, showing forth the Lord's death till he come. It
should secure in its members a visible obedience
to the moral precepts of Christ. It is necessary therefore that the visible church should
provide for the preaching of the gospel, the

administration of the sacraments, and the exercise of discipline. By discipline is meant the admission or exclusion of members upon certain fixed principles, and watching over their conduct so as to assist them in the Christian life by exhortation, consolation, admonition, or rebuke as may be needed.

It might be concluded from the idea of the visible church as representative of the true, that by means of discipline we ought to make the visible church coincide exactly with the invisible, or at least so correspond that every one should be excluded from the visible church who is not a true Christian. But the principle is limited here by the fact that this work cannot be safely entrusted to human hands. On account of human ignorance and imperfection, the visible church is not allowed to attempt to determine who are true, regenerate believers, and who are not. It is allowed to judge the outward conduct and the profession, but not the heart. If a church should attempt by discipline to cast out all who were not truly of Christ's fold, it would not only make mistakes, casting out some who should be retained, and retaining some who should be cast out; but it would also nourish pride in its members, spiritual pride, the pride of the Pharisee. It would encourage them to believe that they were safe because retained in the visible church, instead of leading them to examine themselves as to whether they were depending on Christ. It would be a dangerous error; and so Christ has guarded his people against it in the parable of the tares and the wheat, in which the servants of the householder are not allowed to gather up the tares, lest they should root up also the wheat with them; but both must grow together till the harvest, and then the angel reapers shall gather out of Christ's kingdom all things that offend and them which do iniquity, and cast them into a furnace of fire. Matt. xiii. 24—43.

The outward conduct of church members, however, is to be the subject of discipline. If any man that is called a brother be a fornicator or covetous or an idolater or a railer or a drunkard or an extortioner, the church is to separate him from its fellowship. 1 Cor. v. 9–11. Not that the church members are to refuse all kinds of association with such characters, for then Christians must needs go out of the world; but they are to withhold church fellowship. If any one is disobedient to the scripture rule, the church must note him and keep no company with him that he may be ashamed, not treating him as an enemy, but admonishing him as a brother. 2 Thess. iii. 14, 15.

As the true church is a body chosen out of the world, and visibly separated from it by its obedience to Christ, so the visible church should be separated from the world. For this reason a state church, in which every subject of the state is, as such, a member of the church, cannot so well represent the true church as one that is independent of the state. Though its creed may be orthodox, its discipline will, ordinarily if not necessarily, be lax. It does not afford an outward and visible representation of the line that is drawn between Christ's flock and the rest of the world.

However ministers may proclaim this distinction, it will not be felt as strongly as when
exhibited in a separation between the visible
church and the world, by means of church
discipline. This separation, it is true, may
be seen in the distinction between the Christian nation and a heathen one, as of old in a
contrast between Israel and the Gentiles; but
there is less to remind the Christian nation
now of their distinction than there was in the
case of the ancient Jews; and there is very
little to remind the members of the state
church that among themselves there is a
difference. Even Israel readily lost the distinction between the true Israel and the Israel
after the flesh. In the time of Christ and his
apostles, church and state were disconnected,
not by accident but by divine design. If the
time is to come in millennial days when the
church shall be co-extensive with the nation,
a state church may then be the natural,
necessary, and glorious result; but this must
be by the legitimate increase of the church in
the exercise of its discipline, not by confound-

ing the church and the world. The scriptural idea of the visible church is that of a body separated from the world.

A third characteristic of the true church, that is to be represented by the visible church, is *the unity of the members,* "the communion of saints." In Christ's body, as all the members have a connection with him, so they have with each other; and the visible church should be so constituted as to show forth this truth.

It might be argued from this that there ought to be but one organization, to which every professing Christian should belong; but this principle also is limited by the imperfection of human nature. We cannot make the visible church represent the invisible by bringing every professing Christian into one organization. We must distinguish between uniformity and unity. If we could bring all the professing Christians of the world into one organization to-day, it would not well represent the unity of the true church. Such uniformity could only be obtained by giving up some truth; for errorists, however clamorous

6

for union, would not embrace the truth in
order to secure it, but would require the
sacrifice on the other side. Then when the
uniformity should be obtained, it could be
kept only by the pressure of authority as in
the Romish church. If there were liberty of
thought and speech and action, the discordant
materials would soon represent not so much
the unity of the true church, as the struggle
between the world and the church. According to a familiar principle of human nature,
trivial differences brought into close contact
would be exaggerated, and the materials would
ferment, until there would be division and
alienation misrepresenting the body of Christ.
And if by the pressure of authority the uniformity were maintained, it would not then
represent the unity of Christ's members. The
latter is a unity of faith and love, the unity
of one family, the unity of the members of one
body moved by one spirit, a voluntary, living
unity. The other is the unity of a dead form;
the uniformity of a prison house, where all in
the same dress obey the same authority and

labour at the same work, while hatred may be rankling in their hearts and scowling on their brows; the uniformity of the charnel house, where no discordant sounds are heard—no whisper, even, of dissension, because all is dead. Such has been the unity of the Romish church. The unity that is to represent the unity of the true church should be a free, active, living, and loving unity. There should be in the organization a oneness of thought and feeling, a substantial agreement on all important points, and a charitable agreement to disagree on others. When this unity of thought and feeling exists, then the wider the organization is extended, the better it will represent the unity of Christ's church. It may be too much to expect that all professed believers will ever form one organization with this unity on earth; and it would be mere folly to attempt procuring it by direct effort. Providence at present overrules for good the tendency to division, using it as a means of checking corruptions in doctrine and practice. If unity of organization is to be a glory of the

church in the future, it will be brought about
by the free, unconstrained tendency of Christian feeling, drawing together those who are
brought by the Holy Spirit to think and feel
alike.

It is a proper inference, however, from the
unity of the body of Christ, that whatever organizations may be necessary, should all be
constituted upon the same general principles,
viz., those presented in the Bible. There may
be great liberty and variety in details, while
the representative character of the organization is retained; but this character is destroyed
just so far as any scriptural principle or
direction is omitted or rejected. Hence the
sin of schism lies with that party or organization that departs from the Scriptures, though
it should contain the majority or even the
great mass of professing Christians; and the
true remedy against schism is the conformity
of all to the word of God. Let each organization of Christians aim to conform their constitution and rules as strictly as possible to
scripture principles and directions, and there

will be such a substantial agreement as will
show that there is but one visible church,
as there is but one invisible.

While we should avoid the error of crowding
together discordant materials for the sake of
outward uniformity, we should also guard
against the error of needlessly or wilfully
separating the visible church into disconnected
fragments, and thus denying to those who
have the inward unity of thought and feeling,
the privilege of expressing it by an outward
unity of organization. As the true believer
in one city or state belongs to the same body
of Christ as the believer of a neighbouring
city or state; so in the visible church, if there
be no insuperable hindrances, and no such
diversities of sentiment as would prevent
harmonious action, their union in Christ should
be exhibited by their connection with the same
visible church.   Their unity is not based upon
kindred, neighbourhood, similarity of language
or customs, but upon their common relation to
Christ, and therefore such circumstances
should not be allowed to limit the connection

6*

of Christians with each other more than is really necessary to efficient action. This is the common Christian feeling, the result of the operation of the Holy Spirit. The instinctive tendency to Christian union shows itself in our Conferences, Associations, Conventions, Synods, Councils, and so on; and to repress it because it has been abused, and councils have been perverted into stepping stones to a despotic hierarchy, would be as unwise as to refuse all food because the abuse of food has often laid the foundations of disease.

Besides that a widely spread connection of Christians represents the unity of faith as rising above local considerations, it is the means of efficient action. The men of the world in the prosecution of their schemes, organize and spread their organizations as widely as possible. The church may not throw away such an element of power; and she will not. Whatever theories may be spun to the contrary, it will prove, as in the case of those who inveigh against sects, and soon find themselves forming

a new sect, that those who theorize against
organization will only intensify the peculiar-
ities of their own organization, while others,
if not themselves, consolidate and spread it.
The church, in fact, so far as the scripture
history goes, has never been without an organization extending beyond the local congregation.   Under Moses it had not only its local
organizations, but also its common point of
worship and religious authority for the whole
people.   In John the Baptist's day it had not
merely its scattered synagogues in many
lands, but also its "elders of the people" at
Jerusalem; and the Jews in every country
recognized the Sanhedrim as their highest
ecclesiastical tribunal.   Under the Apostles
it had not merely its local organizations in
Antioch and Ephesus, but it had also a common
bond of union in the apostles, who had
authority over the whole church; and before
the apostles died they taught the churches to
exhibit their unity in the council at Jerusalem.

V.—THE FORM OF THE VISIBLE CHURCH.

The membership—A credible profession—Infants of members not to be excluded—The officers—Rulers a separate class from the ruled—Rulers not to rule singly—To be representatives of the people—Term of office—Power of the rulers only ministerial—Church power valid only when applying scripture principles—Subordination of the parts of the visible church to the whole—Necessary in practice—Authorized in Scripture.

As the church's faith, obedience, and communion are represented in a visible organization ordained by God, we find some principles laid down in Scripture with regard to the proper constitution of this organization, its membership, officers, and form of government.

The *members* of the visible church, according to Scripture, should be professed believers with their infant children. In saying *professed believers* we mean, on the one hand, that a credible profession of faith in Christ, a profession not contradicted by the life, is all that the church can rightly require. It is not authorized to go back of this, and constituting itself judge of the heart, to exclude those who desire to serve and follow Christ, for want of clear proof of their regeneration; although it may and ought to ascertain their views so far as to find that they understand correctly what they are doing. The applicant for membership, indeed, is not to profess regeneration, but faith in Christ. He cannot know with the certitude of consciousness that he has been regenerated, for regeneration is God's secret work and not the object of consciousness; nor can he know his regeneration with the certitude of faith, since *his* regeneration is not a doctrine revealed in the Bible. But he *can* know with the certitude of consciousness whether as a helpless sinner he depends on Christ for pardon and strength; and he can know with the certitude of faith that he who depends thus on Christ shall be saved. He is not therefore to profess confidence in his own character, but confidence in Christ's ability and willingness to enable him to live the

Christian life and secure for him the Christian's crown. That he who does thus trust to Christ, has been regenerated, is certainly true, as we learn from the Scriptures; John i. 12, 13; John vi. 44, 65; but as the faith required for a membership in Christ's body is simply the receiving and resting upon Christ alone for salvation as he is offered in the gospel, so the profession to be required by the visible church is a credible profession of this faith alone.

On the other hand, nothing less than a credible profession of faith in Christ is sufficient in the case of persons capable of such profession. The Scriptures do not authorize the reception of persons into the visible church simply upon their desire to be saved from the wrath to come. Nor is it merely a profession of belief that such a person, as Jesus claims to be, exists, but a profession of reliance upon him for salvation. That such is required is shown by Philip's demanding a confession of faith before baptism; " If thou believest with all thy heart, thou mayest." Acts viii. 37.

That nothing more than a credible profession is required, may be inferred from the fact that the visible church has not the power of ascertaining certainly anything more; and it is plainly taught in the parable of the tares and the wheat.

The infant children of professed believers cannot be rightly excluded from the visible church, if it is to represent the true church. If the true church of Christ contains myriads of saved infants, perchance a much larger part of it consisting of souls saved in infancy than of souls saved in adult years, it could not be well represented by a body which should deliberately declare that infants can have no part in it. And so, in all ages, God has recognized the children of professed believers as standing with their parents in the visible church. They are members of it, not because regenerated, nor because baptized, for they may be neither, but because it is God's will that in the church as well as in the state, the children, until they come to act for themselves, should have the same external position as their parents. Hence Abraham was directed to circumcise his children, and Moses was visited with chastisement for neglecting to circumcise his. Gen. xvii. 10; Ex. iv. 24–26. Hence the Scriptures speak particularly of the children as in the line of God's gracious offers and promises, and of the reception of families into the apostolic church. Said Peter at Pentecost, "The promise is unto you and to your children," much as Isaiah had said, "For they are the seed of the blessed of the Lord and their offspring with them." Lydia was baptized "and her household;" the jailer was baptized, "he and all his;" "also the household of Stephanas." If by the "kingdom of heaven" Christ meant the visible church when he said, "Suffer little children to come unto me, for of such is the kingdom of heaven," then he declared for infant membership in the visible church; if he meant the invisible church, then, as we have said, the organization that represents it, must not exclude little children. Acts ii. 39; Is. lxv. 23; Acts xvi. 15, 33; 1 Cor. i. 16; Matt. xix. 14.

In relation to the *officers* of the church, the Scriptures teach very distinctly both in the Old Testament and the New, that there are to be rulers as a class distinct from the ruled.

The rulers are instructed how they are to rule, and how not; not as lords over God's heritage, but as ensamples to the flock. They are told to take heed to the flock, to act the shepherd to it, and to guard it against wolves. As he that ministereth is to wait on his ministering; he that teacheth, on teaching; he that exhorteth, on exhortation; so he that ruleth is to do it with diligence. Among the qualifications mentioned is that they are to be such as rule their own houses well, having their children in subjection with all gravity; for if a man know not how to rule his own house, how shall he take care of the church of God? The rest are instructed to submit themselves to the Elders. "Remember them that have the rule over you, and submit yourselves, for they watch for your souls." "Let the Elders that rule well be counted worthy of double honour." The scripture teaching on

7

this point is well expressed by the Cambridge
Platform, adopted by the Synod of the Puritan
churches of New England in 1648: "Church
government or rule is placed by Christ in the
officers of the church, who are therefore called
rulers while they rule with God; yet in case
of maladministration they are subject to the
power of the church as hath been said before.
The Holy Ghost frequently, yea always,
where it mentioneth church rule, ascribeth it
to the Elders; whereas the work and duty of
the people is expressed in obeying their elders
and submitting to them in the Lord. So that
it is manifest that an organic or complete
church is a body politic, consisting of some
that are governors and some that are governed
in the Lord."

The power of ruling is in general to be exercised not by single rulers but by tribunals
of associated rulers. It is true that Moses,
Samuel, and others under the Old Testament,
and the Apostles under the New, exercised
power singly; but these were extraordinary
officers, having a special divine commission.

The ordinary rulers of the church, the Elders, are always spoken of in the plural when referred to as ruling. Although in Israel at the people's request the government of Elders was partially superseded for a time by the appointment of a king, God himself selected the king that he might rule as it were in his stead, a visible head to the theocracy, a representative or type of the Messiah; and when the type was fulfilled in the kingship of Christ, and he by his apostles had perfected the reformation of the church, the highest authority in the church, under himself, reverted to the Elders. The Elders, as has been indicated, so far as we can learn both from the Old Testament and the New, never ruled singly. Paul ordained not an Elder but Elders in every church. The wisdom of this provision is obvious. It secures a more careful consideration of the cases that may come up for decision, and guards against a despotic exercise of power. The Elders being equal in rank and authority, no one ruler can rule over the others; and the Scriptural constitution of the church must be laid aside before an ecclesiastical despotism can be introduced.

The rulers of the church moreover are to be chosen in such a way that they may be regarded as the representatives of the people. The officers whom Moses ordained rulers of thousands, of hundreds, of fifties, and of tens, were elected by the people. Compare Ex. xviii. 25, and Deut. i. 13. The seventy Elders whom the Lord directed Moses to take to bear the burden of the people with him, were to be taken from those who, being already Elders among the people and officers over them, were their natural if not their chosen representatives. Num. xi. 16. Though it is not specially mentioned, yet doubtless those whom Paul ordained in every church were chosen by the people, as we know the Deacons were. Since there is nothing said in Scripture as to the time during which the rulers shall exercise their office, it is naturally inferred that they exercise it as long as the people are satisfied with them, and no longer. The nature and design of church authority require that it shall not be exercised over an unwilling people.

The rulers thus become representatives of the people, and are so regarded in Scripture. When God told Moses to speak to all the congregation about the passover, Moses called for all the Elders of Israel and gave the directions to them. Near the close of his life, we are told, Moses said, " Gather unto me all the Elders of your tribes and your officers that I may speak these words in their ears ;" and then it is added, " And Moses spake in the ears of all the congregation of Israel." Deut. xxxi. 28, 30. So throughout the sojourn in the wilderness, Moses and Aaron are said to speak unto all the congregation, which was a physical impossibility unless the two millions of people had their representatives. In David's time it is said, " Then came all the tribes of Israel to David unto Hebron and spake," &c.; which is immediately explained by adding, " So all the Elders of Israel came to the king to Hebron, and king David made a league with them in Hebron

7 *

before the Lord, and they anointed David king over Israel." 2 Sam. v. 1–3. Here the Elders of Israel were manifestly the representatives of the tribes of Israel, who could not well come personally; and the Elders in anointing David acted for the people, since on God's part he had been previously anointed by a prophet. In the New Testament church when the collections were sent to aid the brethren in Judea by the hands of Barnabas and Saul, they were sent to the Elders. While it is according to Scripture that those already rulers should set apart or ordain those chosen, which of course includes the power of refusing to ordain unsuitable candidates, it would be contrary to the freedom which has always characterized the visible church in Bible times, to place the power of choosing the rulers anywhere else than in the people, or to regard them otherwise than as representatives.

The representatives of the people, thus chosen by them to rule, cannot go beyond the laws laid down in the Bible. They have no authority of their own to do so, nor can they derive any from the consent of the governed. The constitution of the visible church is fixed by divine authority and laid down in the Bible. Neither rulers, nor people, nor both, can change it. If they should attempt it, they would simply destroy the claim of their organization to be considered a part of the visible church. Ecclesiastical authority, therefore, is not supreme and arbitrary, but only an authority to administer and declare. In teaching, it can only declare what is the doctrine of Scripture, of which every one must still judge upon his own responsibility; and if, as in the Romish church, it seeks to bind the conscience to believe a new doctrine, it becomes an unlawful usurpation. It cannot, in legislating, require anything as duty which the Bible has not in substance enjoined, but can only make rules and regulations for doing decently and in order what is already required by the Scriptures. In judging, it can receive members according to Christ's law; and in case of offences it can exclude incorrigible offenders. " Therefore put away from among yourselves that wicked person." "A man that is an heretic, after the first and second admonition, reject." 1 Cor. v. 13; Tit. iii. 10. The church has this power in common with every other society, but it can inflict no civil penalties or disabilities.

Legitimate ecclesiastical authority, therefore, is a very simple, harmless, and salutary power. No one need put himself under it unless he choose; and no one is constrained to remain under it any longer than he pleases. If the visible church enacts any thing contrary to the law of Christ, or not taught expressly or by implication in the Bible, it oversteps its powers, and its legislation is unconstitutional, null, and void. Here is the church member's safeguard against the arbitrary power of a minister or a majority. For this reason we say that the rulers do not derive their authority from the consent of the governed. The consent of the members of the Romish church does not legitimate the usurpation of the Pope. The consent of the members of a Presbyterian church would not

give its minister valid authority to preach
Pelagianism or the Unitarian heresy. If an
Independent church should unanimously agree
to make some political or social question a
test of membership, no unanimity of the
members could justify the exclusion of a member for that which is not sinful according to
the word of God, or make such an exclusion
from the visible church valid before God and
the Christian world. In a free country we
may form as many societies as we please, with
what regulations and terms of membership
we please; but no such society can have valid
church authority, save as it conforms to the
rules laid down in Scripture.

It is a scriptural principle that the parts
of the visible church should be subordinated
to the whole. Without this it is impossible
for the parts of the visible church to act in
concert, and therefore impossible to represent
the unity of the invisible church. When
professing Christians are connected together
in a congregation, and a question arises between them, individual opinions and prefer-

ences are to be subordinated (in the Lord) to the judgment of the congregation properly expressed. Thus the apostle Paul teaches that a Christian, having a matter against another, should refer it to those who may have been set up by the church to judge between their brethren. 1 Cor. vi. 1–5. If the disagreement is of such a kind as cannot be settled satisfactorily in the single congregation, they are not shut up to schism, but are to refer it to the representatives of other congregations. So also if two neighbouring congregations disagree. When the representatives of several churches agree upon any point within their proper cognizance, each church should submit to their decision in the Lord; that is, the same principle applies to companies of Christians as applies to individual Christians. If we are to hear with respect the decision of a small number of believers, still more should we hear with respect the decision of a larger body. If any member is aggrieved by the action of the congregation in which he is resident, he ought to have the

liberty of referring his case to a larger portion of the visible church, and one that is un-
prejudiced. This is required by the common
sense of justice ; and in the practical working
of church government, arrangements are
adopted to secure a coöperation of the churches.
These arrangements vary from the most complete to the most clumsy, because the details
are not given in Scripture, but are left to the
discretion of the church. But the general
principle of the subordination of the parts
to the whole we find in Scripture. In Israel
the organization was divided and subdivided
—tribes, families, thousands, hundreds, fifties,
tens ; but they were all united in subordination to the council of the Elders. When the
tribe of Benjamin was nearly destroyed, the
Elders of the congregation consulted for them,
and then commanded them what to do. In
Samuel's day the Elders came to him to ask
a king, a ruler over the whole nation, which
they could do only on the principle that they
represented the nation as a whole. Judges
xxi. 16, 20; 1 Sam. viii. 4. In New Tes-

tament times the church of Antioch, having a disagreement about the obligation of the Mosaic law, instead of trying to settle it among themselves, which must have split them into two churches, a Jewish Christian and a Gentile Christian church, sent their delegates up to Jerusalem with the question. The apostles and Elders came together to consider the matter, and having come to a conclusion, in which the whole church of Jerusalem consented, sent back their decisions. And Paul and Silas, as they went through the cities, "delivered them the decrees for to keep that were ordained of the apostles and Elders which were at Jerusalem. And so were the churches established in the faith, and increased in number daily." * Acts xv. 1; xvi. 4.

---

* The example of the Synagogue in New Testament times, though it cannot be taken as authority after the rejection of Christ, will serve to illustrate the constitution of the Christian church which was evidently derived from it. . Saul's authority (Acts vii. 14.) to persecute in Damascus was derived from the High Priest at Jerusalem (Acts ix 1) acting as moderator or executive officer of the Presbytery. Acts xxii. 5. "The great Sanhedrim

VI.—THE PRESBYTERIAN FORM OF CHURCH GOVERNMENT.

Church power vests not in the clergy but in the people—Comparison with Episcopacy—The Presbyterian way preferable—Officers representatives of the people—Conformity to the Scriptural plan—Church power to be administered by Elders—Comparison with Independency—Disadvantages of the latter —Independency modified in practice—Advantages of having a bench of Elders—Puritan views—Presbyterian Eldership different from Episcopal—Meaning of "Bishop" in Scripture—Several Bishops to one parish —Testimony of Episcopal writers—Apostle Bishops—Origin of Diocesan Bishops.

THE foregoing chapters have taught that the visible church is a representative of that true church which consists of those who are

claimed over the Jews in foreign cities the same power, in religious questions, which they exercised at Jerusalem." Conybeare and Howson, Life of St. Paul. i. 81.

8

saved, or are to be saved, through Christ, and
that it is designed to represent its faith, obedience, and unity; that the visible church
should have for its members professed believers with their infant children; that it
should have rulers, ruling not according to
their own will, nor by their own authority,
nor in ordinary cases singly, but according to
the laws of Christ, as representatives of the
people, and associated in tribunals; and
finally, that the parts of the church, so far as
practicable, should be so connected, and so
subordinated to the whole, as to express the
unity of believers.

These principles we find recognized more or
less fully in the different forms of church
government actually existing; though it may
be that none perfectly exemplifies the true
ideal of the visible church, even as no single
professing Christian perfectly exemplifies
Christianity. Without going into an examination of all these forms, the Presbyterian
form will be considered, as being the one that
we prefer, and will be elucidated when neces-

sary by comparison with the others. We
shall classify our remarks by connecting them
in the present chapter with the characteristic
principles of Presbyterianism as to church
power—where vested and how administered;
and in the next chapter with the Presbyterian
principle as to the relation of the local congregations of professed Christians to each
other.

The first principle of Presbyterianism in
regard to church power is that it vests not in
the clergy, but in the whole body of believers.
To elucidate this, we may compare Presbyterianism with Episcopacy. In the Protestant
Episcopal church in the United States the vestry
are the representatives of the people, and appoint deputies of their own number to the
Diocesan conventions, where a Bishop presides,
and clerical and lay deputies have an equal voice.
The Diocesan conventions appoint clerical and
lay deputies to a General convention, but the
influence of the lay deputies here is diminished
by the fact that the house of clerical and lay
deputies can do nothing without the consent

of the house of Bishops. Through the house
of Bishops, therefore, the clergy have control
over the legislative power of the church. In
matters pertaining to the discipline of the
congregation or parish, the reception or exclusion of members, the laity have no power.
Discipline is in the hands not of the vestry
but of the Rector, whose responsibility is to
his Bishop. In the Methodist Episcopal church
in the United States, the power is virtually confined to the itinerant clergy. There are no lay
delegates in the Annual or General conferences.
Those only have a voice in them who are
under the direction of the Bishop counselled
by the Presiding Elders. They are not the
representatives of the churches—not even
clerical representatives, for they are not chosen
by the churches, but sent to them. A case
of discipline may be referred by the "Preacher
in charge" to a committee of the church
members chosen by himself; and whether
tried by the committee or otherwise, if the
member should appeal, his case goes to the
Quarterly conference, consisting of the Pre-

siding Elder, the preacher in charge, the class
leaders, stewards, exhorters, and local preach-
ers of the circuit, none of whom are appointed by
the people, but all appointed directly or indi-
rectly by the itinerant clergy. Even the
property of the society is held in trust for the
use of the preacher who may be appointed by
the conference.

In the Presbyterian church the Pastor,
Elders, and Deacons hold their office by the
choice of the people. In the government and
discipline of the congregation the Ruling Elders
are the responsible body, the clergyman having
no vote save a casting vote when the session
is equally divided. The Ruling Elders, though
not laymen, since they are ordained to an
ecclesiastical office, are properly representatives of the laity, since they are not constituted
by their occupations, education, and mode of
support, as clergymen are, a separate class
from the people. In all the courts above the
church session, the representatives of the
people have an equal voice with the clergy.
In receiving and licensing candidates for the
8 *

ministry, and ordaining, trying, and deposing clergymen, they have their vote, so that the clergy is not a self-perpetuating body, but is perpetuated by the representatives of the churches. These representatives may be chosen for a year, as in the Scotch church originally; or for two years, as in the Reformed Dutch church; or for an indefinite period, as is the common custom. They are not chosen, as is sometimes asserted, to act for life, whether the congregation continues satisfied with them or not. The constitution of the Presbyterian church provides for their ceasing to act, if they become unacceptable in their official character to a majority of the congregation, though they may be chargeable with no fault. They stand in this respect on an equality with the clergyman; as long as the congregation is satisfied with them, they act without a re-election; and in this permanence of the office there is a safeguard against the assumption of undue power by the clergy.

The energy and promptitude which the

Episcopal plan of government can give to the movements of the visible church, may well be admired; and so long as it is the plan of but a small part of the visible church, while the great body secures the rights of the people, it may not be very dangerous.   Yet the Presbyterian plan which secures those rights of the people, or rather the rights of the Lord Christ entrusted to his people, is to be-preferred.   The practice of vesting church power in the clergy naturally leads to the principle that it belongs to the clergy of right; and this as naturally leads to clerical encroachment and abuse of power.   It was by gradual steps in primitive times that the officers of the church lost their character of representatives, and became lords over God's heritage.   The principle that church power belongs to the clergy of right, involves a great error, any approach to which is dangerous.   For on what ground can church power be rightly vested in the clergy as distinct from the people, save this, that they are viewed as special depositaries of the Holy Spirit?   If it is in the people that the

Spirit of Christ dwells, then the rights and powers of the church belong to the whole church. If, however, the Holy Spirit is given to the clergy, and comes to the people only through their ministrations, then indeed the power of government should belong to the clergy, for the church ought to be guided and governed by the Spirit of Christ. They should determine what the church is to believe and profess; who shall be received, and who excluded; who shall teach, and who shall be taught; for their decisions are dictated by the Holy Spirit. This is the claim of the Romish clergy, and it is consistent with Romish doctrine. Here too lies their tremendous power over the conscience. If they are the depositaries of the Holy Ghost transmitted by succession from the apostles, then separation from them is a sin against the Holy Ghost; it is schism and rebellion. In their hands is salvation, and to reject their authority is perdition. It is consistent, therefore, that all church power should be placed in their hands.

It is not to be supposed that Protestants

hold this arrogant assumption of the church of Rome, save, of course, where the assumption is boldly avowed, and we are told in plain terms that those who refuse obedience to the so called apostle-bishops, have no claim, however pious they may be, upon God's covenant mercy. But it should be understood that vesting church power in the clergy, as distinguished from the people, cannot be justified except upon principles that lead to such dangerous conclusions.

The Scripture doctrine is that the Spirit dwells in all believers, making them one body, and giving to each member his appropriate gift for the edification of the whole. All believers have an unction from the Holy One, by which they know the truth. Epistles with directions for church government and discipline are addressed not to the clergy alone, but to the saints with the bishops and deacons, or simply to the saints. Private Christians are thrown upon their own private judgment and told to pronounce even an apostle anathema if he should preach any other doctrine. The

practice of the early church was conformed to
this view. When an apostle was to be added
to the eleven, the two from whom the Lord
was to choose one by lot, were elected not by
the eleven, but by the disciples numbering
about one hundred and twenty. The election
of deacons, though they were not rulers,
indicates the same principle; if the apostles
would not appoint officers to manage even the
temporal affairs of the church without an election by the whole multitude, there is no reason
why they should ordain spiritual rulers without it. The Synod of Jerusalem to which the
church of Antioch appealed, spoke on behalf
of the whole church. Though it was the
apostles and elders who came together to
consider the matter, their decision was agreed
to by the whole church, and this is mentioned:
"Then pleased it the apostles and elders
with the whole church to send chosen men of
their own company to Antioch." And the
letter containing the decrees said to have been
ordained of the apostles and elders which
were at Jerusalem, and delivered to the

churches for to keep, begins with the words,
" The apostles and elders and *brethren* send
greeting." Acts xv. 22, 23. The principle
recognized in the Presbyterian form of government, that ecclesiastical power resides in the
whole body of the church, and not merely nor
mainly in the clergy, seems to us to have been
very distinctly recognized by the apostles,
and to have the sanction of divine authority.

The second principle of Presbyterianism in
regard to church power is, that it is to be administered by bodies composed of elders or
presbyters. Here we may elucidate it by a
comparison with Independency. The latter is
a pure democracy. There are no rulers.
There may be one officer in each church to
teach or preach, who is called an elder, but
even he is not a ruler. The elder or minister
has in theory no more authority than any
other member of the church. But, as has been
shown, the Scriptures command Christians to
obey them that have the rule over them, and
submit themselves, because they watch for
their souls; and it speaks repeatedly and in

various forms, of church officers as rulers, and
of church members as ruled. Presbyterianism
follows the Scripture plan by having rulers in
each congregation to secure an orderly government, while it preserves the rights of the
people by making the rulers their elective
representatives. The responsibility of discipline is thus concentrated, and the power is
at the same time guarded against abuse.

The Independent theory is far less practicable
than the Presbyterian, as well as less scriptural. While it gives the minister no more
authority than any other member, in actual practice almost the whole burden of responsibility
devolves upon him. As no one member more
than another is personally bound to have discipline exercised upon erring or unworthy
members, the minister, if he would not have
his labour wasted, must see to it that discipline
is exercised. He must therefore arouse the
church to attend to it, and whether the offenders are sustained by the church or condemned,
the burden of the odium must rest upon him.
It is easy to see that discipline is specially

liable to be neglected under such circumstances. Moreover, when the church is prompt to act, there is danger of haste, rashness, and injustice. Some cases need secrecy. It is not always proper that the details and proofs of a scandal should be exposed before a promiscuous assembly of males and females, old and young. It is not always best that the offence should be published to the world; the evil may be made far worse, and the offender hardened by the exposure. Nor is such a promiscuous assembly, where the feeling of personal responsibility is necessarily weak, well suited to weigh testimony and try causes, even though consisting of professing Christians. A large assembly, made up of all grades of intellect and all varieties of prudence or imprudence, is scarcely fitted for a jury, and much less fitted to act as judge, deciding questions of law as well as fact. Such a body is very liable to be swayed at pleasure by an eloquent and popular speaker or one accustomed to act as a leader. In fact, as a pure democracy is ever in danger of becoming the

9

government of the demagogue, so pure Independency is ever exposed to clerical usurpation.

A government of this kind, it is plain, would not be suited to the wants of new converts from heathenism, except as its defects were supplemented by the personal influence of the missionary. Nor would it satisfy us in civil affairs. If on the commission of a crime it should be the business of no one more than another to bring the offender to justice, but the schoolmaster or any other public-spirited person is to volunteer to ring the bell, and the township is thereupon to assemble in town-meeting to inquire into and try the case, adopting their own rules of procedure, with no appeal from their decision, we should consider it a very rude form of government, ill adapted for civilized society, and too much resembling "Lynch law" to be generally adopted.

Pure Independency is consequently but seldom consistently reduced to practice. Even those who are attached to the theory, frequent-

ly adopt Congregational usages, which are an
approach toward Presbyterianism. Such a
usage is the appointment of a judicious standing committee to prepare business for the
simple approval or disapproval of the church,
or the giving somewhat of the functions of
spiritual rulers to the deacons. Something
of the kind is needed in all large congregations,
if the government is to be well conducted.
Said the eminent Massachusetts congregation-
alist, Cotton Mather, in speaking of the watch
and care of a congregation, " And they must
allow me that this work is too heavy for any
one man, and that more than one man, yea
all our churches, do suffer beyond measure
because no more of this work is thoroughly
performed. Moreover they will acknowledge
to me that it is an usual thing with a prudent
and faithful Pastor himself to single out some
of the more solid, aged brethren in his congregation to assist him in many parts of this
work on many occasions in a year; nor will
such a Pastor ordinarily do any important
thing in his government without having first

heard the counsels of such brethren. In short, there are few discreet Pastors but what make many occasional Ruling Elders every year." He then proceeds to argue for the regular election and ordination of Ruling Elders by the churches.

Upon the Presbyterian plan, the church chooses the Pastor's assistants; they are all made of equal rank with the Pastor or Preacher, and each has an equal voice with him; they are solemnly set apart and ordained to bear rule; they cannot but feel a personal responsibility for the purity of the church; they constitute an effectual safeguard against any undue clerical influence; and both the church and its rulers have a clear conscience and a firm faith in carrying on the government, inasmuch as they regard themselves not as practising devices of human expediency, but as conforming to the plan laid down in Scripture.

That it is according to Scripture to have a number of Elders in each congregation was the doctrine not only of the continental and

Scotch Reformers, but also of the English Puritans. The Westminster Assembly declared for it. John Owen, the great champion of Congregationalism in England, contended for the Ruling Eldership with unanswerable arguments from Scripture. The Pilgrims' church of Amsterdam, besides having three Deacons, a Pastor and a Teacher, had four Ruling Elders. Among those who landed from the Mayflower upon Plymouth rock, was Elder Brewster, a Ruling Elder. Nor was this an exceptional case. The Massachusetts Synod of 1648 says, in the Cambridge Platform, "The Ruling Elder's office is distinct from the office of Pastor and Teacher. Ruling Elders are not so called to exclude Pastors and Teachers from ruling, because ruling and government is common to these with the others; whereas attending to teach and preach the word is peculiar unto the former." The article on Congregationalism, prepared at Andover, Mass., for the Religious Encyclopedia, says, "By the early writers of New England and the Cambridge Platform, the officers of

9 *

the church were Pastors and Teachers, whose
duties were distinct ; Ruling Elders, like those
of the Presbyterians ; and Deacons, who
looked to the temporal interests of the church
and provided for the poor. For· all these
officers they claimed the sanction of divine
authority."

The present lack of Ruling Elders, therefore, in the New England churches, is a de-
parture from the old ways, while it is no improvement. Though some New England
writers now seek to justify this destitution of
the churches, they do not appeal to any
scriptural arguments that were not known to
their fathers. Formerly the destitution was
lamented. The Synod of 1679, in answering
the questions, " What are the evils that have
provoked the Lord to bring his judgments
on New England?" and, "What is to be
done that so many evils may be removed?"
said, " It is requisite that the utmost endea-
vours should be used in order to a full supply
of officers in the church according to Christ's
institution. The defect of these churches on

this account is very lamentable ; there being in most of the churches only one teaching officer for the burden of the whole congregation to lie upon. The Lord Christ would not have instituted Pastors, Teachers, and Ruling Elders, (nor the apostles ordained Elders in every church,) if he had not seen that there was need of them for the good of the people. And, therefore, for men to think they can do well enough without them, is both to break the second commandment, and to reflect upon the wisdom of Christ, as if he did appoint unnecessary officers in his church."

Cotton Mather, in his Ecclesiastical History of New England, published in 1702, says, " There are some who cannot see any such officer as what we call a Ruling Elder directed and appointed in the word of God ; and the inconveniencies whereinto many churches have been plunged by Elders not of such a number,* or not of such a wisdom as were desir-

* The error of having very few or only one Ruling El-der in each church, appears to have led to the disuse of the office. The responsibility and the odium of discipline

able, have much increased a prejudice against the office itself; be sure, partly through a prejudice against the office, and partly, indeed chiefly, through a penury of men well qualified for the discharge of it as it has been heretofore understood and applied, our churches are now generally destitute of such helps in government. On the other side: there are others who if they are asked, what order for lay Elders in the word of God? answer, that properly the only *lay* Elders known to be in any church, are the chancellors in the church of England, persons entrusted with the rules of the church, and yet *not ordained* unto any office in it. But that unless a church have divers Elders, the church government must needs become either prelatic or popular; and that a church's needing but one Elder, is an opinion contrary not only to the sense of the faithful in all ages, but also to the law of the

were too little distributed, and hence arose disinclination to accept the office, and dissatisfaction with those who exercised it.

Scriptures, where there can be nothing plainer than Elders who rule well and are worthy of double honour, though they do not labour in word and doctrine ; whereas if there were any Teaching Elders who do not labour in the word and doctrine, they would be so far from worthy of double honour, that they would not be worthy of any honour at all." Dr. Dwight, of Connecticut, says in his Theology, " Ruling Elders are in my apprehension Scriptural officers of the Christian church; and I cannot but think our defection, with respect to these officers, from the practice of the first settlers of New England, an error in Ecclesiastical government."

Would it not promote the orthodoxy, piety, peace, and stability of the churches, if the error to which Dr. Dwight alludes, were remedied by a return to the government of Ruling Elders ?

Presbyterian government by Elders or Presbyters differs from Episcopal, in that Episcopal Elders take a rank inferior to the Bishop, rule singly over the congregation or parish, and are not directly representative of the people. In the Presbyterian church there are several Elders or Bishops to one congregation : in the Episcopal church there is but one Elder (the Rector) to a congregation ; and there are several congregations, each with an Elder, under one Bishop.

Presbyterians hold that there is but one order of permanent Ecclesiastical rulers, that of Elders, warranted by Scripture,—the Deacon not being a ruler, but ordained to attend to temporal affairs ; and the term Bishop, or overseer, being only another name in Scripture for Elder, designating one of his principal functions. The word Bishop occurs five times in the New Testament. It is used by Paul in addressing the Elders of Ephesus : " The flock over which the Holy Ghost hath made you Bishops" (Overseers). He uses it in addressing " the saints in Christ Jesus which are at Philippi with the Bishops and Deacons ;" where we see that there was a plurality of Bishops in the church at Philippi as well as at Ephesus. He tells Timothy the qualifications for a Bishop: "A Bishop then must be blameless,"&c. He mentions the same qualifications when directing Titus to ordain Elders in every city, and adds, "*For a Bishop* must be blameless;" which shows that by Elders and Bishops he meant the same officers. In the fifth instance where the word occurs, it is applied by Peter to Christ, the Shepherd and Bishop of souls. Acts xx. 28; Phil. i. 1; 1 Tim. iii. 2; Titus i. 6; 1 Pet. ii. 25.

It appears, therefore, that in apostolic times each church had several Bishops. From the fact that there were several in each church, we might readily infer that they were not all set apart to attend exclusively to preaching and worship, much less to oversee subordinate clergymen. It would be impracticable, or at least impolitic, to have several clergymen to each church. And it appears from Scripture that a part of the eldership was designated in each church to labour in word and doctrine, 1 Tim. v. 17; not, as we think, to exclude the rest from such labour, but by concentrating the responsibility to secure the punctual, orderly, and edifying performance of the duty. The elders were all " to bishop" (oversee) the flock, all were worthy of double honour, but only a part, say one in each church, laboured in word and doctrine.   The bishop thus set apart for preaching would naturally be made the mode- rator or president, and would soon come to be known as emphatically *the* Bishop, while the other bishops would be known as simply pres- byters or elders.

Both the existence of the Ruling Eldership in the primitive church and the equality of bishop and elder, are granted by eminent Episcopal writers.   As one of many, Arch- bishop Whately in his "Cautions for the Times," says, " A bishop in the primitive ages was the chief minister of a particular church, and had no ecclesiastical superior on earth. . . . And a bishop in these times was not the sole spiritual governor of the diocese over which he was placed, but he presided over a council of elders, who in concert with him managed the affairs of his diocese. . . . . A deacon, again, in early times was an officer who had

charge of the church money, and who was in-
trusted with the task of dispensing it to the
poor. But with us, you know, those parts of
what was the deacon's office are generally
devolved upon others."

Since Episcopal writers grant these points,
on what ground, it may be asked, do they
defend the claim of their bishops to oversee
many elders and churches, and the course of
their church in dispensing with Ruling Elders ?
Some defend it on the principle that the form
of church government is very much a matter
of expediency, and that the Episcopal form is
the most expedient; to which we answer that
we cannot think any form of government expedient which is not conformed to the scriptural model as closely as our circumstances
allow. Others defend it on the assumption
that the modern Episcopal bishops are the
successors not of the New Testament bishops
who were but elders, but of the apostles ; and
that they inherit the apostolic authority over
the church. This claim of apostolic authority
we answer as we do that of the Pope to be.

10

Christ's vicar on earth; we deny the validity of the claim and ask for the proof. If they have the authority of the apostles, we admit that all should obey them; that all who refuse obedience are out of the true church and in peril of damnation; and that as true religion would produce obedience to apostolic authority, there can be no true religion out of the church that is subject to them. But this claim, with these tremendous consequences, is entirely unsupported.

It is not necessary to show the difficulties and absurdities involved in the doctrine of apostolical succession; it is enough that it is unproved. The whole Protestant church, except a part of a single denomination in this country and Great Britain, has rejected the claim of apostle-bishops; and for aught that appears, that part of the Episcopal church which rejects " apostolical succession," has at least as much appearance of true Christianity as that which defends it.

It is true that while we can find no proof in Scripture of any permanent order of rulers

higher than elders or presbyters, of whom
there were several in each church, and some
of them not set apart specially to labour in
word and doctrine, we find in the church of the
middle ages, and indeed from quite an early
period, elders subjected to the government of
Diocesan bishops. We have sufficient evidence
however that in the primitive church for some
time after the death of the apostles, the scriptural plan of government was retained; and
we can easily see how the primitive eldership
came to be lost. As the church became popular and prosperous, it became corrupted.
The work of discipline, as it became more
needed, became more odious. The people did
not like the business with which the ruling
elders were specially charged; nor did the
elders like it themselves. The sluggish wished
to be rid of the care and odium, and the
ambitious preferred the office of preaching
elder. At the same time, as a church grew
large, instead of forming new churches from
it, each with its board of elders, it would be
districted into parts each under the charge of

one of the elders, and all under the superintendence of the preaching elder, who was emphatically *the* Bishop. This arrangement would gratify the ambition of the presiding bishop to retain a large church, and the ambition of the ruling elders to become preaching elders; and it would satisfy the people who did not wish for the exercise of discipline. Thus the bishop of a city church would soon come to have several congregations and their presbyters under his oversight, and the ruling eldership would be soon extinct. And so, St. Jerome, who wrote within three hundred years of the apostles, and had every opportunity to know, tells us that presbyter was originally the same as bishop, and the churches were governed by the joint council of the presbyters; that afterwards one was elected to preside over the rest as a remedy against schism; and that by little and little the whole concern was devolved upon an individual. Thus the whole system of church government was gradually changed into the Romish hierarchy; and the Scripture plan of government by a council of elders was preserved through the dark ages only by such scattered bodies as the Waldenses and Bohemian brethren, until the Reformation.

VII.—PRESBYTERIANISM—*Continued.*

Union of the local churches in one church— Comparison with Independency—Congrega- tionalism—The argument against Indepen- dency—Difference between Presbyterian and Congregational practice—The Consociation more efficient than the extempore council— The Presbytery has the advantages of the Consociation and more—Presbyterian gov- ernment gives a better safeguard against heresy—It is completely adapted to the mis- sionary work—Conclusion, Ecclesiastical re- publicanism.

IN the Presbyterian form of church govern- ment the local churches are intimately con- nected with each other, being united for gov- ernment and discipline into one church. In this it does not differ from the practice of the great body of the church in all ages. To

10 *

illustrate it by contrast we must refer to Independency, according to which each particular
congregation is a complete religious common-
wealth entirely independent of all others. It
has something in common, with others, and
may associate with them, as France and
England have something in common, and may
associate for certain definite purposes; but a
member of the one local church does not
thereby obtain any rights or interests in the
others. He can no more appeal from the
judgment of one to the others than a citizen
of the United States can appeal against a
decision of an American court to the British
Parliament.

On the Presbyterian plan all the local
churches or congregations are united, as the
townships of the United States are united
under one system of government. As each
township has its own government, but all the
townships subordinate to the county; each
county its government, but subordinate to the
state; each state its government, but subordinate to the United States; with written con-

stitutions defining the powers and rights of each department, and a representative system running through the whole; so the local churches, each with its Board of Elders to govern it, are united in subordination to the Presbytery; the Presbytery is subordinate to the Synod; and the Synod to the General Assembly; while a simple system of representation runs through the whole, and the powers of each part are limited and defined by a written constitution. The humblest member of the smallest Presbyterian congregation is thus a member of the whole church; and if his rights should be infringed, he may appeal from the judgment of the single congregation to that of a larger portion, and, if need be, to that of the whole body.

The Congregational form of government, as distinguished from the Independent, approaches toward the Presbyterian. It recognizes the common interest of all the churches in the character of the clergy, and in the purity of discipline in each. It holds the rightfulness of an appeal in cases of discipline from the particular church to a council of the representatives of the churches, though it clothes the council with merely advisory power. It sanctions associations, consociations, and conventions to concert measures for united action in preserving and propagating pure doctrine. Its agreement with Presbyterianism was formerly even greater in this country than it is now. In England, whence the settlers of New England came, the scattered bodies of dissenters from Prelacy had not the opportunity of systematizing a scriptural church government on a large scale, as had been done in Scotland; and among these settlers there was doubtless a leaven of Brownism, or Independency, which had risen out of the recoil from an arbitrary Prelacy; but as a body they believed in the communion of churches as well as in the communion of saints. The Cambridge Platform says, " Synods orderly assembled and rightly proceeding according to the pattern, Acts xv. we acknowledge as the ordinance of Christ; and though not absolutely necessary to the being, yet many

times through the iniquity of men and per-
verseness of times, necessary to the well-being
of churches for the establishment of truth and
peace therein." A subsequent assembly of
ministers at Cambridge, elucidating the Cambridge Platform, declared that "there is the
light of nature as well as of Scripture to
direct the meeting of churches by their delegates to consult and conclude things of common
concernment;" that " Synods duly composed
of messengers chosen by them whom they are
to represent, and proceeding with a due regard
unto the will of God in his word, are to be
reverenced as determining the mind of the
Holy Spirit;" and that " all the commands
of God which bid us to be well advised and
regard a multitude of counsellors, do particularly oblige us with reverence to entertain
the advice of Synods assembling in the name
and fear of the Lord Jesus Christ for an en-
quiry after his directions. And if one church
be to be heard, much more are many churches
to be so, in things that properly fall under
the cognizance thereof."

The Synod of Boston in 1662, in answering the question propounded to them, "Whether according to the word of God there ought to. be a consociation of churches, and what should be the manner of it;" defined the duties of churches to each other, among which they specify: "In love and faithfulness to take notice of the troubles and difficulties, errors and scandals of another church, and to administer helps (when the case necessarily calls for it), *though they should so neglect their own good and duty as not to seek it.*" Says Increase Mather, "That the churches of New England have been originally of the Congregational persuasion and profession is known to every one; their platform does expressly disclaim the name of Independent;" and says Samuel Mather, "The churches of New England are nominally and professedly Congregational. They do not approve the name of Independent, and are abhorrent from such principles of Independency as would keep them from giving an account of their matters to their brethren of neighbouring societies, regularly demanding it of them."

The churches of Connecticut tired of the irregularities of previous practice, early adopted the plan of standing consociations instead of extempore councils; and the Saybrook Platform (1708) holds that any church which does not regard the decisions of a consociation shall be considered guilty of contempt, and that an act of non-communion shall be declared. The Connecticut plan, if carried out, is so far Presbyterian. Of late years however, a party has arisen, which tends to weaken the authority of the consociation, and defends what the fathers of New England deplored.

Presbyterians and Congregationalists, as distinguished from Independents, argue that the church of Christ according to Scripture is one body, all parts of which are subservient to the growth and prosperity of the whole: the body is joined together and compacted by that which every joint supplieth. The gifts of the Spirit are given to a believer, not for his own benefit merely, but for the benefit of

the whole body of Christ. They are given to
a company of believers for the same end. A
believer or a company of believers independent
of the body, would be like an independent
finger or an independent ear. The visible
church was constructed by Christ to represent
this truth. No congregation is intended to
exist for itself alone. No professor of religion
nor body of professors is right in needlessly
separating from the rest of the visible church.
When a man becomes a true Christian, he
joins the body of Christ—the whole body of
true believers the world over ; and not merely
the believers in his own village. When he
becomes a professing Christian he ought not,
by joining a congregation of professors in his
own neighbourhood, to be cut off from the rest
of his fellow professors elsewhere, with whom
it is practicable for him to live and labour in
church fellowship. The essential condition
of his membership is not his residence in a
particular locality, but his agreement in the
profession of faith. If through local prejudice
or otherwise he should be aggrieved by the de-

cision of this particular congregation, he ought to have the right of appeal to the church at large in some representation of it. Every church moreover has an interest in the settlement of questions of doctrine and discipline by every other. If one church tolerates heresy or immorality, all the others, and especially those most akin to it in doctrine and order, suffer with it. It is therefore as necessary that churches should unite their counsels for investigation and decision, as that individual Christians should do so; and such decisions are binding in the one case as in the other—no less, no more. Accordingly the Scriptures give us an account of the settlement of the dispute in the church of Antioch by the Synod of Jerusalem. In the words of Dr. Dwight, "As this judicatory was formed under the direction of the apostles themselves, it must be admitted as a precedent for succeeding churches; and teaches us that an appellate jurisdiction is both lawful and necessary in the church."

As to the necessity and duty of having an appellate jurisdiction, the great body of the visible church is agreed. The mode of its administration, of course, varies with the general form of church government. The Congregational mode is most nearly allied to the Presbyterian, yet it differs from it in some respects ; and the Presbyterian practice which is fixed and uniform, while Congregational usage is various, furnishes, we think, a system that is more efficient and reliable. In case of difficulty in a Congregational church, the usual course is for the aggrieved party and the church, or the minority and majority, to agree to call a council composed of a minister and delegate from each of several churches, one half being chosen by each party ; or if the majority will not grant an appeal to a council, then the aggrieved party may call an ex-parte or one-sided council, chosen entirely by himself. In either case, after the council's decision the church or majority may do as it pleases, though usually the advice of a mutual council will be regarded.

In a Presbyterian church the appeal or complaint is taken to the presbytery, a permanent body consisting of one ruling elder from each church in a certain district, and all the preaching elders—a body whose constitution and rules of procedure are published and well known, and which is itself amenable for the regularity of its proceedings to a higher court. The Presbytery confirms or reverses the decision given by the bench of elders who, under the name of Session or Consistory or Parochial Presbytery, govern the particular congregation. If either party considers itself unjustly treated by the decision, it may appeal to the Synod, representing a still larger section of the church; and from that to the General Assembly representing the whole denomination. While a council can only *advise* the church to restore an unjustly deprived member to his privileges, and the church may refuse to do so without forfeiting its standing, the decision of the Presbytery secures the restoration of the member, and the church must acquiesce or appeal to a higher court, or leave the Presbyterian body. The Presbyterian mode of appeal, therefore, gives a more effectual safeguard against the prejudices and tyranny of a local majority.

A Presbytery is likely to be a more impartial tribunal, and therefore to carry more weight of influence, than an extempore council. A New England writer, describing the state of things in Connecticut before the plan of consociation was adopted, says, " As there was no general rule for the calling of councils, council was called against council, and opposite results were given upon the same cases, to the reproach of councils and the wounding of religion. Aggrieved churches and brethren were discouraged, as in this way their case seemed to be without a remedy. There was no such thing in this way as bringing their difficulties to a final issue." Said the great theologian of New England, Jonathan Edwards, " I have long been perfectly out of conceit of our unsettled, independent, confused way of church government in this land ; and the Presbyterian way has ever appeared to me most agreeable to the word of God and the reason and nature of things."

Dr. Dwight, after showing the necessity of a tribunal of appeals, says, " Such a tribunal in all the New England states except this (Connecticut), is formed by what is called a select council; that is, a council mutually chosen by the contending parties. This has long appeared to me a judicatory most unhappily constituted. The parties choose, of course, such persons as they suppose most likely to favour themselves. If therefore they commit no mistake in the choice, the council may be considered as divided in opinion before it assembles, and as furnishing every reason to believe that it will not be less divided afterwards. Its proceedings will frequently be marked by strong partialities, and its decisions, if made at all, will not unfrequently be those of a bare majority. Coming from different parts of the country, it will have no common rule of proceeding. After its decisions its existence ceases. Its responsibility vanishes with its existence, as does also the sense of its authority." After other similar remarks, he adds, " In this state (Connecticut), a much

11 *

happier mode has been resorted to for accomplishing this object. The tribunal of appeal is here a consociation; a standing body; composed of the settled ministers within an associational district, and delegates from the churches in the same district; a body always existing; of acknowledged authority; of great weight; possessed of all the impartiality incident to human affairs, feeling its responsibility as a thing of course; a court of records, having a regular system of precedents, and from being frequently called to business of this nature, skilled to a good degree in the proper mode of proceeding. The greatest defect in this system, as it seems to me, is the want of a still superior tribunal to receive appeals in cases when they are obviously necessary."

It will be seen that the advantages justly claimed by Dr. Dwight for the consociation over the extempore council, are the very advantages possessed by the Presbytery; and that the defect complained of in the plan of consociation, is supplied in the Presbyterian

organization by the Synod and General Assembly. It should be added, however, that
while the authority of the Presbytery is among
Presbyterians unquestioned, that of the consociation among Congregationalists is not so
generally admitted.

Congregational and Presbyterian churches
agree that each church is interested in the
purity of its sister churches, and may withdraw fellowship from those that are here-
tical in doctrine or lax in discipline. Presbyterian practice, we think, gives a more
efficient means of preserving the purity of the
churches than is afforded by Congregational
usage. It brings the representatives of the
churches together statedly and frequently to
inquire into the condition of their churches
and consult for them. As in a single
congregation the watch and care of members
will be better attended to, when a bench
of elders is set apart for that purpose
and made responsible for it, than when the
responsibility is left with the congregation at
large; so the watch and care of churches will

be better attended to, when devolved upon a permanent body with its stated meetings and regular examination of church records, than when lying loosely upon the neighbouring churches, who will not meet in council until called together by some special effort. In the Presbyterian system, if a church, to avoid the trouble of discipline, tolerates scandalous heresy or immorality in its minister or members, or does injustice to a member whose ignorance or obscurity may discourage him from making an appeal, it is likely to be known to some member of the Presbytery ; and when that body comes together at the stated time, if not before, it has the right and is under obligation not merely to examine the church records to see that what discipline it exercises is carried on in regularity and justice, but also " to visit particular churches for the purpose of inquiring into their state, and redressing the evils that may have arisen in them."

Congregational usage provides no such efficient means of nipping evil in the bud. Though the reputation of the churches may

be suffering and the poison spreading, the evil
goes on until it becomes notorious and un-
bearable, and then the neighbouring churches
may withdraw from fellowship. The poison,
however, may spread very widely before this
can be done. Rev. Z. K. Hawley of Norwich,
Connecticut, in giving reasons why Unitarian-
ism did not spread in Connecticut as in Massachusetts, says, " But in Massachusetts, if a
church or candidate for the pastoral office was
corrupt in doctrine, it was comparatively easy
to select a council from among those who
were infected with the same error; and thus
the leaven would spread in secret till it had infected the mass." The history of the Unitarian
defection in New England is a sad commentary
on the inefficiency of Congregational usages.
Without the work of the Holy Spirit, indeed,
no system of any kind, no excellence of
machinery, no perfection of mere means, can
secure the visible church against the influence
of human depravity; but while humbly depending upon the divine power for results, we
think that the combination of order and free-

dom in the Presbyterian system, the security
of individual rights, and the efficient protec-
tion of the churches against error, mark it
out for our adoption as the best means that
the divine word and providence afford.

The Presbyterian plan presents superior
facilities for carrying on the great work of the
church, its missionary work. With this plan,
the visible church needs no apparatus independent of itself or extraneous to it. Its
government can be set in operation among
newly converted pagans as well as among
those educated to self-control. Where a church
democracy would be anarchy, and a church
monarchy would be too near an arbitrary
despotism, elders can be ordained in every
church, and Presbyteries formed, and the
simple but strong machinery of a republican
government will prove a valuable means of
culture. At home, too, the church under
Presbyterian government finds itself equipped
with all the means necessary for carrying on
the work. All its operations are strictly
under its control, while all parts of the church

and all classes are fairly represented. The education of young men for the ministry, the choice of men to go forth as missionaries, the publication of books and tracts, the erection of church buildings, and the collection and disbursement of funds for these purposes, are all managed by the representatives of the churches. The whole church is a missionary society, transacting its business in its Congregations, Sessions, Presbyteries, Synods, and General Assemblies with their various committees and boards. It needs no societies or agencies outside of itself to do its work; and since Christ and his apostles established no such society or agency, that plan of church government is surely preferable which makes the visible church as such competent to labour under his last command.

In reviewing the characteristics of Presbyterianism we are reminded of the analogy it bears to republicanism in civil government. While other forms of church order may be found analogous to Monarchy, Aristocracy, and Democracy, these principles—that the power vests in the people, that it is to be administered by rulers representing the people, and that the different parts of the church are to be subjected to the whole—clearly mark this form as the Republicanism of the church. In the providential progress of free institutions, the science of civil government has attained a high development ; but its highest development has simply brought mankind, after many centuries of turmoil and bloodshed, to that system whose principles are all laid down in the scriptural constitution of the church, and were exhibited in ecclesiastical history, while a true representative republic was yet in civil history a thing unknown. With all its imperfections, the visible church, so far as it conforms to Scripture doctrine and order, is the main organic agency for human improvement; and it is so because it is the representative of a redeemed and new-created humanity, the body of Christ.

CPSIA information can be obtained
at www.ICGtesting.com
Printed in the USA
BVHW03s1454170518
516550BV00009B/69/P